Courtesy photo: Shabnam A. Danesh

Stars Light: Stem & Leaf

SIXTH VOLUME

Abol Hassan Danesh

Order this book online at www.trafford.com
or email orders@trafford.com

Most Trafford titles are also available at major online book retailers.

Courtesy photo: Shabnam A. Danesh

Printed in the United States of America.

ISBN: 978-1-4269-6706-1 (sc)
ISBN: 978-1-4269-6707-8 (e)

Trafford rev. 05/04/2011

 www.trafford.com

North America & international
toll-free: 1 888 232 4444 (USA & Canada)
phone: 250 383 6864 ♦ fax: 812 355 4082

Contents

DEDICATION

For Fatemeh

Principal (Late) Fatemeh Bigom Hajseyedjavadi Danesh

Mother, Libertarian, Royal, Visionary, Pioneer, Faithful, Brave, Resilient, Simple, Joyfull, Kindhearted

Introduction

In close parallel with the fifth volume of stars light's theme and content, Stem and Leaf Volume, is an attempt to put the entire six volumes of stars light poetry in perspective. Perhaps a comet would be a better metaphore to capture the spirit of this volume of work in terms of its connectivity potential to the continous & long taill blazing of light from the point of its origin to that of destination. That is, a clear demarkation of territory travelled through stars light journey. In simple words, another way of looking at the milky way in heaven, is to see it as a large star comet itself in standstill with all trail light path way travelled made visible in close up. And for further illucidation of this volume may I then suggest that the stem of a leaf is itself the trunk of tree par excllence, making sure the leaf never leaves the tree despite all the falling, break away, and separation in each year and in each and every other season.

I take this opportunity to thank the entire trafford publishing company team for working with me on this bumpy and protacted road toward the publication of not only this volume but also the previous one as well.

AH Danesh

Narragansett Rhode Island

April 21, 2011

—About the Author—

A.H. Danesh is a professional sociologist by training. Doctor Danesh picked up poetry later on in life as a self taught & self-recreational intellectual activity with substantial borrowing from his sociological knowledge background. In addition to writing poetry, Doctor Danesh enjoys gardening, hiking, & short distance running on his long list of hobbies. This volume is the last volume on the long & distant trail of stars light poetry. This journey of mind and heart took him nearly over a decade, and resulted in nearly one and half thousand pages of published work, that began with his father Danesh stars light first volume, and ended in rebirth with mother Fatima (lily) the sixth volume now before the eyes of esteemed readers toward their benefits for birth, reflection & regeneration.

Books from Author:

1. Rural Exodus & Squatter Settlements in the Third World. 1987. University Press of America.

2. The Informal Economy: A Research Guide. 1991. Garland Press.

3. Corridor of Hope: A Visual View of Informal Economy. 1999. University Press of America

4. Stars Light. First Volume. 2004. The Author House

5. Stars Light: Second Volume: Flame of Life. 2006. Air leaf Press

6. Stars Light: Third Volume: The Evening Dew. 2008. Mountain Valley Publishing Company

7. Stars Light: Fourth Volume: Sheila: Love Must Be Loved. 2008. Libras Publishing Company

8. Stars Light: Fifth Volume: Leal. 2010. Trafford Publishing Company

Leaf

Love

One

Another

As

I

Have

Loved

You

Or

Else

You

Will starve to death

With breakfast, lunch and leaf dinner

In heaven for ever beyond your reach

Sky Tree

From the high up sky tree

Snow flake stars gently falling

Each omes cwith exact six symetrical edges

Despite their endless variety in whiteness

Just like the falling leaves in autumn

With their endless colors, shapes, and forms covering the earth

But with stem attached as their common denominator

From the memory of their parents

The snow flakes covering the fallen leaves of yesterday

With thick and warm blanket

Until they all desolve back to soil as fine stems

In deep sleep soaked in heavenly water of stars light

Sixth English Curve

Inside the English word "world"

The word "lord" is written in scrambling

To stress that

In pursuit of Lord

One may not forget the significance of world affairs

Lips Leaves

A lovely perfumed lavender woman

Has two leaves each on her lower and upper lips

But she closes her mouth

Then she has only one lip but far a bigger and engorged one

This is the horizontal one

Worth suckling every bit of it

There comes the vertical lips in the middle world

That no one knows

Who and for what and for whom and why

One is suckling up to

And for what reason

However, regardless of the vast interpretations of it

The vertical and the horizontal leaves

Are going to make a "T" shape

With generous amount of grace space

Between the upper and the lower lip leaf

Beyond man logical mind for interpretation once set on fire

Winterizing Poetry

The autumn has ended

The trees all are naked

The echo of traffic now has a different sound

These are true sign that

We have become winter bound

The spirit of winter demands man

To become all wrapped up

Like trees full of leaves

When the fall had not begun

I search for amazement during the shortening days

I search for amazement during the lengthening nights

I find reading and writing poetry quite fine

There is music in some poems

Filling winter air vacuum like warm blanket

When all the leaves are gone

Primary Colors

It is cold early spring

My golden delicious apple tree

Is all barren naked leafless

Too early to have its leaves shoot out

Along with its pinkish perfumed buds in blossom

Hosts a bird on one of its branches

To empower man's source of imagination

Yes, the bird is the apple size vibrant red male cardinal

What is the story?

The story that now it is the early fall

And the last red apple

Is still dangling in midair

Resisting Newton gravitational force

With all its might

The Dew Ascension

The Last night dew

Had been sitting on the roses and roses leaves in the rose garden

Now gently evaporating in steam

Like the breath of joy

Ascending to heaven in dance in slow motion

Under the warmth of too early morning spring sun rays

As it working itself out through the last night chill

Morning dew now ascending to heaven

In the early morning dew

In vapor and in joy

Still the lush green lawn in shade is carpeted like the Milky Way

With endless translucent diamond dews in brilliance

Greed Is Good: Always More Room Left to Eat

Leaves of Bread

Are left unattended

While the starving people

Devouring the leaves of money

In the lifeless barren desert of greed

With no hope in sight

If they ever get fed

To leave this table

In contentment

Seen and Not Seen

I am wind

When I blow you see me through leaves

As they move and begin to talk to you

I am wind

You see me when I move the cotton clouds in sky

In their ever changing images for the fun of children

I am wind

You see me when I move the ship

I am wind

When you can't see me for I am many

Acres of Cherry Blossom

Cherries' blossoms are amazing

They shoot out way ahead of the green leaves

Turning the tree

Into a bride from head to toe covered in white garment

And then begin to descend like snow flakes in dance

From the body of cherry blossom bride

Carpeting the earth in white satin snow

Day in and day out for weeks

Under the self confident hot solar rays in rising temperature

Yet they hardly melt

And constantly bees and rare birds

Come touching smelling the brides' mild perfume

Asking where the grooms are hiding

Star Bow

My bright daizies

Have exploded in light

On the top of thin but tall branches

Like constelation after constation of stars in the milky way

But the yesterday heavy rain

Had been too hard on them during the reign

Thus some have bent all the way

To touch the green lawn.

They now are land stars in bow

While still connected to their roots in the milky way

Entrapped Moisture

I planted the first tree

The second, the third

Now I sit back and look at them

With their intense competition for position and place

Pushing their roots ever deeper into the soil for survival

Oh I love the damp moist

That gets caught between the spread out leaves

Reminding me that I have succeeded to make forest

Right in my back yard

You may call me Mr. Squirrel

But the one that brings diversity

When planting core and seeds without expectation for return

Oh this entrapped moisture between the leaves

Is so promising in attracting more rain to come

Going Behind the enemy's line

The time unit of the Angel of death

Is split second

But Man's is second

And despite being way ahead of

This rabbit's split second

The rabbit will eventually

Catch up with the turtle man's second. ...

Thus a wise turtle man second

Always works behind the the rabbit split second

Until the turtle second gets caught up

By the rabbit half second

After the rabbit

Has completed the run

Around the earth.

That works in split minute and half second

Danesh's Law Engraved onto hard rock

We all want to get rich and stay beautiful

With no looking back

But know before hand

The passage to this end

Is as tight as the tunnel inside the hair line

Thus with this well scrutinized law many will perish without a whisper of

nagging

Therefore be ready for death and suffocation

Before the run for wealth begins...

In Defense of the Gullibles

Man's tongue is the machine gun

With masterful access to

The bullet amunication dictionary and the right choices of words

He can literally turn his audience brain into a sieve

En route their ears toward total surrender

Therefore, in order to counter this assualt

When there are abuses of this deadly arsenal

Is to imagine youself a massive rock and the bullets are the popcorns

Bouncing up and down on you

Toward your entertainment and nothing else after the show is over

Bones of Horrific Beauty

In human body

There are three places that the savage barbarism and sublime civilization

Meet one another in a joint common ground

Toward joint reinforcement

His bloodless & crucified nails; his crucified hairs; and his crucified teeth

As long as these three barbaric civilization oxymorons know that

All the three of them are hosted by soft humane tissues

We might be ...

"Beesetoon"

Magnificent ceilings

Taller than any known palaces made by man

Docorated with endless bulbs of light at night

Standing on its own

Without the support of any known standing pillars

As fresh air moves in and out in perfume

This ever high ceiling is the roof of man's only shelter

Build to save him from the demon

That is lurking somewhere in the outter space and beyond

Kicking

In late december winter time

It was a nice warm day

For conversation,

I went to the woody sitting on the naked tree without leaves

Asked him

Why you have grown such vibrant red feathers

Only on the back of your head

He laughed and said

It is a communication sign

Which means, when lord signals you something

It is only an incomplete sentence

And with your hot and active head brain of yours in kicking

You m... You m...

Deep Minds in Deep Union

It was me and it was me again and the flower

Three of us sat together

We did not utter a word for quite a long while

Until a friend came by

To sit with us to continue the same conversation

We had left in triad in utter silence

Stitches

If you think you can stitch the broken heart

In the same way you can stitch the broken body

Then you need to think again

For the former is the work of god without payment

While the latter the work of man

Who must get paid in advance

Upon showing your insurance card before visitation

Perfume

Fresh apple unskinned

Is an open jar of perfume

In it still intact the essence of its promised spring blossom

Upon its coception

As a promising child

But orange!

You must cut through its thick skin with bare hand or sharp knife

So it can open up its sealed off jar of perfume in generosity

Of course with all the mist in explusion

Orange after the cut

Wish to be treated as an equal to apple

Now that its perfumed water dropping all over the places in plenty as hard

evidence

Best Wishes

Shooting star

High above in heaven

Born in light

Live all the way in light

In straight path without interuption

Then die in light only to disappear

Be happy now

All the frustration

Disappointment

Dismay

And your great sense of anger

Will all vanish and come to an end upon your death

Close your eyes

Inhale and exhale gently

As you step inside the corridor of death in slow motion

January Thaw

Man is a giant icicle

And from genuine exercise

Sweat may begin to roll down from his eyebrow to the ground

Like a melting icicle during the January thaw

But dripping is deceiving

For in few short hours

The cold will set in

And with it

Only the icicle man to get a bit thicker and colder to emerge

From what he was before the thaw

Staying there like a tall standing statue of Ice in long freezing cold

Yes indeed we all need reliable refregerator.

To keep us all away from ruins, rotten spoil, bad oder, and corruption

Wish

The season of fall has arrived in full swing

Trees one after another have become naked without the wings

Their leaves falling down toward earth

Just like the shooting stars but with songs and sings

But what is it that these shooting stars are singing?

Yes, Hassan what do wish now that you are in the ring?

My reply to the shooting leaves stars mounted into only one word:

The ever green

Untitled

My best written poem is a blank page

Showing off to my ancestors

They just can't fool me

With their half baked scribbling on the stone wall in a damp cave

To tell me

They preceded me and they were before me

Yes, you figured it all right

The title of this poem is "Mute"

Greatest Fish on Earth

The gentle pristine clean river

Flow slowly & quietly

On a flat shallow floor in earth runway

It is all trarnsparent

Inside out in a sunny day

And the reflection of the waves on river bed

Looks like fish's scales without end

The giant river fish is about to enter the giant ocean

Body

Feast of mind has depth like a thick book of poetry

With table after table of food back and forth

All compressed to one another without gluing

But the feast of body has only one page

And on its backside there is nothing meaningfuly edible found

That one can speak of with confidence

An Illiterate Love Dove

A blank leaf of white page

That hasn't been yet poisoned

With the ink of poet

And yet not being raped

By his erected lustful cock pen

Is a clean unscratched window

Opening to the fresh world of spirit

Where a white sweet love dove

Leaves a dark room

For the fresh air of heaven

Without ever looking back

Unit of Love

A lone petal breaks away from the flower

Falling...

Not only to annouce its independence in loneliness

But also its meaning...

Still a thin leaf in essence with stricktest diet

While wrapped in colors of love

Deadline

A bare stark tree

With all its naked branches

Apears as human brain

But when leaves worn later on

It becomes a grown up brain

Then that's the brain hard at work on a project with an stern deadline

Blank Page The Tabula Rasa

It is so sad

To see man with friends

With family members

Who has written or read pages after pages of books, magazine,

newspapaer

Or has given interesting speeches

But once dead

They only scrible few words on a flat stone in piercing in hurry

And then put it on top of him

To summerize his entire life time journey achivements

For folks who come visit him to witness

What he has been doing all these years

When he was busy walking on earth

Some even become more unfortunate

Thrown into mass grave like Mozart

With no sign of his world achievement whatsoever

For live world for viewing

Future

The moment the child is borned

The best husband is dad

The best wife is mom

As mom and dad focus on the future

The way to hold on to their union

With it to navigate

Into the unkown

Into the promisng stars filled milky way

Road is closed: It Is the Deal Stupid

You go to the poor

They speak of injustice and betrayal

You go to rich and to the super rich

They also speak of injustice and betrayal

You go to the priest

To the proletariat, to the beaurgeoisie

To the king in his glittering palaces

They all too speak of injustice and betrayal

However the moment you find them dead

With red blood pumping still thourhgout their body

Then you see Suddenly

The topic of coversation shifts to contentment and union

Intravenous

After some miles of running

The sweat begun running down

From my eyebrow

To the ground

In slow motion

One drop at a time

Just like the gentle drops of intravenous entering the patient body in coma

Upon receiving these drops during my two hours of ICU hospitalization

Rolling down from head to toe

I surely got up from the death bed

Toward somewhat of a recovery

A Poem for Remembering

The blue ocean roars and roars and a little more

Up and down in wave to keep on pour

Even it sometimes go over the board

To make a little pot hole lake

Like a little core

The overflow sometimes

Flows like a river.

That later on come back

To join the ocean while in roar.

Just a little reminder for the vast ocean in gore

Not to forget its humble beginning

Like a poor river in bend and bow flimsey and careful in soar

Recycling Rum

On the sand beach

With Ocean waves crashing on the shore

Laid down empty large rum bottle

Wind blowing onto the bottle making sounds...and says…

Oh as a defender I once held the Rome together intact

But they found a way to get into my sealed head

They finished up the juice of my oath

They drank up the spirit of my resolve

Now I am only an empty shell drifting

Hoping someone to pick me up again

To throw me back in the hell fire of recycling

So at least a tiny piece of me

Could go to make a bottle

With head sealed holding the Rome intact once again in vow

How to Smoke Science

Any given ideology

Is like a hose

Punctured at few places

And regardless of which tape or glue is used

To seal off the holes

With increased water pressure of truth

The hose is bound to leak

More and greater

Just like a typical ideologue

Who keeps constantly suppressing?

The cropping up of anomalies

By making up ever more unusual stories

On the verge of stupidity and mental madness

For cover up

Will Power

For Vanessa

I was thrilled once I saw

My friend had given a rare gift to my daughter on her birthday

Yes inside a cute red brick size automobil

Both radio and CD player had been placed beautifully

Speakers installed as car front tiers

With ease to stir the wheels around for better listening

Other day I spotted a fancy man made wooden Roaster

Inside of which a cool fan was housed

For while

I felt main feature of the post modernism era

Was juxtaposition of two different entities side by side

But now only will power

Ruins

Man should hang a framed picture of run down home and shack on his

wall

So as he refurbishs

Enhances

Upgrades his place of residence

Slowly and gradually

To a respectable clean cut home

With all the work and labor spent

Always to remember his roots

When he looks at that picture once in a while,

To make sure he has not evolved into a rude privileged exclusionary hood

Blood of Messiah on Soil

Man spends much of his time

Build himself

Better and greater shelter

All the way until his shelter

Metamorphoses into a glittering mansion

But the irony is

His permanent residence at the end

Ends up being outside of his own beloved residence

--The graveyard--

Eavesdropping

She asked me

To read more books

To improve my vocabulary

To enhance my options for presentation

So my poetry could become

More dazzling and more attractive

In response I told her

Dear I write poems not for an audience out there

But for myself from within

Like a bubbling musical fountain

Flowing right inside of a dark hard rocky mountain

And as far as this person is concerned

I enjoy every bit of it

And hope the audience as well

If they choose to put their ears on the mountain

For eavesdropping

To Prolong the Prolonging

Some weeds

Have learned

Over the long course of adoption and survival

To redress themselves

As leaves of flowers

But the thing is

No matter how long the gardener waits for them

They only grow and no news of flowering but frowning

This is the time that

The uprooting hands of patient gardener

No longer get fooled

By the camouflaging

Diaper

I love

a poem a child writes

while sitting on his parents' lap

pressing the keys on the computer

in utter randomness in giggles & excitement

Of course...

Once the child's work is done

Print the baby's work

Hang it from the wall

inside a nice expensive glass frame

to see what heaven was replaying to the baby

in utter classiness while pooping in his diaper

Okay...okay.... I heard you

The parents can help the baby in his art work

Holding and releasing the shift and the cap lock

to improve the quality of art work tied to paradise

Moments: Feeling Impoverished

No matter how many times

You have eaten from open café

Spreading their colorful tasteful tables of food and drinks

Ever farther into the street for great visibility

You feel inferior as if you are from a lower caste

Even if for only once you pass by them

Not having enough money in your pocket

To eat out in its hustle and bustle of publicity

Surely man is utterly forgetful

When it comes to leisure and good time

Odor & Germ

When see the neighbor

Letting their dog

Come leaving its waste in your yard

Don't go to them asking:

Mom, Is this your dog

Coming to my yard ...

Instead ask correctly

Is this you who is coming to my yard keep ...

For when it comes to waste

All carnivores' waste are the same

And unlike the vegetarians

They all spew bad repulsive odor

Attracting lots of nasty flies spreading germs

Natural Denture

Ever time

I skin a good size ripe mango

Eat it like a savage to the end

I reach its large hard core

I feel as if I am wearing a bony denture

Came out of my mouth

Having hard time to put it back

In order to get back

Natural feeling of my own teeth

I go ahead skin a kiwi

Eating it all the way to the end

Now I have my denture back in my mouth

As natural as any human being can feel

Inside the Bunker

Strong wind blowing in relay summer...

Large and small trees

All bend and bow in music

And their branches full of green leaves

Move back and forth in an unease awakening in agitation

Some even break apart to descend

With the season of fall still way far in the background

Nonetheless...

The roots remain in standstill

Unshaken in the deep dark

holding their ground

without yielding to the wind

even for a tiny bit compromise

In Rib

I

Am

That

the

Thy Poor

who lives in

Glorious glittering glory

with the shine outshining

all the shines emanating

from all the kings' palaces

Throw out All your astronomy books all at once

For your face

Is the full moon

That has just about to be risen in the east

For your eyebrows

Are the crescent moon only few days old

For your nose

Is the submit of mountain

Connecting to its mountain range cheeks and the outskirts

For your eyes with sparkles in them

Are those bright winking stars

And your ears are the spiral milky way

Of which the earth is only a tiny part

Of course your open lips in open happy laughter

Are the sun itself in a happy autumn day

Thy your chin is the little or big dipper

Which of course depends on

Size of your dimple with its awesome whirlpool power

Finally your forehead

Is the large kindergarten book

That I have ever been opening up in full

Before your star eyes in awe

Do I need to go on further to say

The pen will go to construct which part of your body

Or should I announce class recess right now?

Tall Stems

My sound is strong!

So when I sing my opera song

In front of tall wheat stems in big golden farm in autumn

They all bend backward when I exhale my breath sound for assertion

As I inhale for renewal they all bend forward

The ones staying behind me

All stand in stand still for continuous standing ovation in silence

Throughout the performance

Of course if I get lucky

To have no sudden tornado around

To blow at the field of farm life thousand times stronger

For a counter punch

Gullible Children

Butterfly on its wings

Softly flies and sings

That if kids

Touch hiss's flowers

That they will get

My big stings

The butterfly is joking

He knows there is no power in his things

Yet the kids don't touch hiss's flowers

For they have been taught

The butterfly has huge painful stings

Ever Lasting Fire in Mid Air

My fence rose

That comes in deep red

Has matured

Well into its graceful old age

With branches

Spreading all over the fences

And I am laying down in lush green grass in late spring

Watching this mega red fire in hanging

In air in smokeless perfume

Wondering...

When this blazing fire place in suspense

could ever completely extinguish

as some of its fire petals

gently separates, breaks away and descends on earth

in utter softness & humility

Hats Off

What

Better hat

One can put on

Than the hat of education graduation

And then once worn and pictures taken

Begin to throw it all up in air in hurray

To ecology not only the sweet freedom

But also some room for the hat of ignorance

Without which life as we all know it

Is inconceivable

Questioning...

After I saw

In Michelangelo's painting in Vatican

All the lovely angels

Surrounding the God

In a closely knit communion

And then compared my loneliness

To His most famous lone

I said to myself

This is not God who is all by himself alone

But myself who is far away from the communion of

Both Demons and the angels

Now the question is

What God does with these lovely angelic sweethearts

When all the lights are turned off at night

No question! God must be more handsome than all of us!

Fun: Order is good but...

From order

There comes the intimidation and horror

And of course the more perfection of it

The greater horror it will muster under its belt

Thus if you wish to make friends and more friends

Particularly from the social class of less fortunate

Learn to mix that order of perfection with some sense of chaos

For as far as order and chaos is concerned

There is no limit to each side of the spectrum

When the war breaks out

The death of an Ax man

He dies

From only one mortal sin

He keeps chopping up

What lies

Only underneath him

Even though in English language

The ax man

Must chop up

Instead of chopping down

Pristine

I live in a village

With streets have no names

The passing cars have no plate number

Houses devoid of number identity

When people want to find the address

They look into signals being given off

In the written calligraphy of frosting

On leafless branches of trees in winter

In awesome shapes of leaves as they in star constellation on earth

Tell you what street you should not go into

In sounds of birds as they move from one tree to the other

To give you a tentative map that must be completed

By your own imaginative improvisation

At the end when you get to me in this village

You must have been so intoxicated by such musical road finding

Only to be found in my door steps unconscious

For the overdose

Funny Sparrow

A typical brownish sparrow

had gone on the top of a tree

with full white & pinkish blossom in a sunny day in spring

singing his best song

ever he could come up with

what is he singing

I have dream...

A day that I could sing as sweet as a finch in love

I have a dream ...

A day that all birds are listen to carefully

I have a dream ...

A day that I could finish my singing journey

Now that I have taken my first step

I have a dream...

To break from my spryness rank and free

Frowning Face Revisited

Ever time I see a man saying after his meal:

O thanks Lord

I am now all fed and content

feed those who are hungry

I tell myself in laughter:

O what a lie...

For man's stomach throughout his life time

is like an endless abyss well

and it will never ever get filled

Even if he has eaten up to the rim

His most delicious lunch or dinner

in row and for few weeks in fine dine

Hear it in Persian: We are on the same team

The Europeans

Started and then finished

Two painful world wars

And dragged the entire world into the conflict

only to figure

"It" was only all about the money stupid

However there are few countries left in Europe

who still resist

accepting this way too simple and stupid euro solution

well...

Let's wait and see

if they can pull off the Rabat

Along with flying love dove

Right out from their cute purse to show off

their intelligent trick

for overcoming the world conflict

--jaguar yore many--

I Am Reigning Now/

Despite

All the will power

I put in managing

A cluster of grape

while devouring it in an standing posture

At least one breaks free from the grip of my dominion

Falling in an incredibly slow motion on ground saying:

Remember this

Part of me must become wine

This is my heavenly destiny

That must be fulfilled

Beyond and above your will power

Variety: Expanding on Greek Mythology

Today I spotted

A brownish female sparrow

But with golden head of a finch

Surely a rare breeding

And after some thought and reflection

I told myself

When man cannot find his lover on his own term

His choices for mating is surely limited

Particularly when he is in rush

And has no time

To consider optic for birth control

O well ... who knows

Charles Darwin might have had a different take

Hot House

Remember

No matter

How grand and beautiful one's house is

He must get out of it

For fresh air and spirit

Only available out in public

Or else his splendid house

Becomes an equivalent of hunted run down shack in shantytown

Filled with the spirit of demon

In entrapment

Now having said that

Improve your place of residence bit by bit

Or move to new location for a new shake up

ID: The Computer Key Board Identity

Virgin

it

carries

Sixty eight signs

Mounted on forty seven keys

to stress the fact that

in the world of scarce resources

every bit of saving space

by going vertical

Is counted

to avoid uncontrolled sprawling

into the virgin hinterland

is a great virtue

Worth pursuing

by nails

If not

Tooth

Seagull the Teacher

The river was transparent and cool

The seagull after so much search & navigation

Flew few feet high and then dived

To catch the detected crab under water with his sharp beak

Surprise ...surprise ...

Sat next to me unusually way too close

Only to begin to devour the food

Surprise ... surprise...again ....

The Henry seagull left few small pieces behind

only to fly up in search

to catch more living creature for food

but why did the hungry seagull left

some small pieces behind?

Yes, it is customary when you eat your meal with company

you don't lick the place to the last fiber

before heading once again

for business to find the food

Naked Heaven

Sky is the tree

Its tiny leaves are the stars

And they are falling

In acrobatic dancing

In abundance

Like a windy day in atom

With excess leaves up in air flying

And when these wintry bright leaf flakes

Descend on earth

They cover the naked trees

As their heavenly leaf dress in light

To keep her ready in full attire

For the anticipated wedding ceremony

At the expense of

Keeping the heaven tree naked

Stripped of most if not all their star leaves

The One: Long Stem

I took out

My favorite

Dried out

Maple leaf

That I was hiding it for long sleep

Between the pages of

My favorite book

Now I let the sun shine

Touch the leaf on its "edge" straight through

With its shadow now casting

On my favorite book

In a shape identical with its own stem

But quite longer

I put the flattened leaf

Back in its book bed again

With all the lights off

Toward its long uninterrupted sleep

Why Abraham Lincoln Was A

I

Am

Not

Against

Giving

Freedom

Liberty

And pursuit of happiness

To the slaves and to my subservient

As long as in the process

They don't come back

To claim my freedom, liberty

And my pursuit of happiness

Simply said

There should be put in place a mechanism

Before hand

So the liberated won't Push their Luck too far!

Ground Zero

What kind of world we are live in?

What kind of world?

It has become all materialistic

Devoid of spirit

and in order to reach the material

Man slit another man's throat

as comfortably as

He cuts cheese for breakfast without thought

yet the unit of this beloved material

On which he builds his aspiration for wealth and more body

That is right is the penny

And it is spread like dog drops in street

Yet no body bothers to pick it up

To put it back in his piggy bank

For time of emergency

Then one wonders

Where materialistic folk's ties are

When you don't find them bending

"To pick it up"

Help make their dream come true

With a solid base intact and unshakable

Treasury Department

I

Have hung

A bird feeder from the tree

As small birds poking at the holes for the seeds

For every single seed they devour

They drop several seeds on the ground

To say out loud:

You should be generous to others

By sharing your food to the less fortunate

Particularly when your food itself

Came to you free

Straight from the treasury department

Being a Dead Horse: Legitimate Brutality Revisited

The Greatest

Folly of modern man

Is to test and retest

Again and again

On the dead man

To find

The bottom line of endurance

From which to build a new recorded standard

A crystal clean "Case"

To apply to common man

As legitimate

As legal

With recorded proof

Obtained in objective experimentation

Horror of Urban Landscape

An outdated digital camera

I inherited from my daughter

After some play

The camera stopped working altogether

Thus I began to break up the camera

Like a little boy in curiosity

With mud and worm dangling from his mouth

What I found inside the box though was amazing

On its little platform

There was a miniature map of

Miniature Traffic Intersection,

Homes zoning, gas station, business district, etc.

All appeared with small tiny wires routes in camouflage

With invented dots of melted lead

Juxtaposed to one another so closed

Indeed it was the map of large megalopolis urban sprawl

Right under my stunned and gazed up eyes and mind

What I left with after the camera break up

Was the idea that who the grand master was?

And who were the workers who put this amazing structure

On the back of a tiny brownish thin slate

Piano Teeth

Her lovely laugh

In a beautiful sound

In a gentle exhaling

Appeared on a set of

Long and extended white teeth

All in perfect order

Inside her all opened up mouth

At first I thought

I am looking at the piano keyboard

All in crispy shiny white

With a music identical to human sound

When he is in an absolute happiness in jubilee

Absolute Icicle Wrist Watch

From the tip of long & extended icicle

Drips of diamonds

Gently falling on the ground

Under the pleasant warm sun rays

Just like the minute hand of

My wrist watch

Except at uneven interval

Stressing the fact that

The same amount of time

Can be experienced and felt

Differently in duration

Depending upon zillions of things

Happening in the Cosmo

In interaction with one another

Or in standstill

My friends when it comes to find the accurate time

With great precision

Forget the Swiss watch

Instead look for crispy diamond icicle watch

It even works and shows time accurately

When time itself is frozen

Illiterate

I

Planted

Several morning glory seeds

In a pot full of nutritious soil

With couple of sticks inserted in there

Now after couple of months passed

In cold winter freeze

When everything is frozen

Except the evergreen trees

Every now and then

I see one or two of them in full bloom

In a surprise delight

Like finding a guest from paradise

Waiting for you from behind the window

In an splendid colorful attire

In green skirts

That spell the word "love" for the illiterate

Submit at once!

Man

Has gone to moon

Man has invented electricity and computer

Man has made awe braining medical break through

Man has invented TV, Radio, and Telephone

Man has made endless list of impossibilities possible

But has fallen by the way side and miserably

To combat his arch enemy to bring him

under his whim and control

Threatening his very existence on the planet earth

Ladies and Gentlemen it is not the global warming

But surprise...

It is the number of babies he brings to life

when he is involved in

hotly hot affairs in full penetration

in an equally hotly hot bed in utter forgetfulness

of all the rest of human consideration

Hot Soup

It was winter

It was cold

It was windy

It was brutal but beautiful

It was a sunny day

It was covered with snow

I walked for hours

Icicles were hanging from my long mustache

In between

I passed by a house

With the chimney in full swing

The smell of burning wood

Blowing toward me from distance

Was the greatest perfumed

I had ever smelled in my entire life

I was warm ... it was inviting...

I felt right at his home before his fire

yet with all wood smoke perfume intact within

without a bit of it escaping to the outside world

when I reached my home

I felt the spirit of Lord in warmth

had filled the entire space in an immaculate silence

Luxury Hotel as Class Room

If

Someone

Has been keep snubbing you

With his house

Take him to a luxury hotel

To snob him back

And if still he has not learned his lesson in humility

Threaten him that

you might next time

Take him to see

The glittering shining palace of the emperor

For after all

Home is made for man for his rest

Regardless how humble

Some of them are constructed

Little Laugh at the Speed of Light

I

Am

God

All there is in the universe

All reside within me

All galaxies reside within me

Nothing exists outside of me

Time does not exist

Speed does not exist

For they are only man made creations

Sprang up from his primordial self-deficiencies

from which he will never recover

For he needs job and more jobs

Post

When

You see

So many

Baseless, rude, corrupt and arrogant individuals

Have come to fame and honor

In public life

Rest assure that

There are as many great original men of honor

Have been berried in the dungeon

Without letting the world

See their light

Indeed!

Joseph has been thrown into the well

by the insignificant evil doers

In order to beef up their own resume

Indeed!

Slow Motion

There is warm fire power

In the crowd

In the social gathering

In the partying

In the intermingling

And then there is warm fire power

In being alone

In being in silence

In being in isolation

In being in meditation

In being alone thinking

Imagining...Imagination...

And if you are locked in the second category

yet without fire

you then better do something

Even if it means to beg

and spend all your saving money

to join the first category

Or else you will freeze into death in slow motion

in a deep depression

Can They Improvise?

Some folks

In gang society

Speak so self assured

Using only the very extreme tip of their tongue end

To impress others and show their brevity

While keeping the rest of it virtually idle

Except for food swallowing

You wonder what will happen to them

if in an accident

They lose that small tip of their tongue

Isosceles sand time

From

The sharp edge of icicle

hanging in suspense from the roof

Fresh crispy transparent tiny ball of water

just like a sweet rounded diamond

in slow motion dripping down...

But as it drips

The length of icicle itself increases slowly

Despite the meltdown

Like a sand time box

Except as it tics in drip down

You get more sands

Accumulated in the upper floor of glass time sand box

Wage the need of invasion

To let the sand time flow further in the future

Awaiting for Total Victory

Infinite whiteness

In form of white snow

With the depth

Enviable by any floating iceberg

This infinite whiteness

Coexists peacefully as equal with

Infinite darkness

For almost six months

In the north pole

Until this coexistence of the two equals

Shifts to the south pole

But I tell you this

With the increasing global warming

At the end

The darkness wins the whiteness

Regardless for how long more

The aurora ornaments the sky of north pole

With its dazzling colors in delightful light

Take Side Before It's Too Late

There are

Two kinds of running

A man who runs

To kill another man

And a man who runs

To save the life of a man

Just in the same way

The wind blows in the season of fall

To put the trees in sleep

And the same wind blows in the season of spring

To awaken the sleeping trees back to

life

Just in the same way the same rain

Brings death and life

Depending upon in which season

It is pouring...

Ho ... Santa Clause Coming to the Town

The way

Almost all human society is set up

Has the tendency

To turn man's heart into the stone

That is to live in society

Is to become stone heart

For man must interacts to survive

In close ended and close minded rings

But thanks to all the human festivities and celebration

Scattered throughout all the four seasons

Work as shock therapy

To revive the stone heard

From the dead to the living

And to restore his heart once again

Imbued with spirit

Land Stars

The yesterday last night fluffy snow

has descended

from heaven to earth

with it of course

the plenty of stars of sky

have landed also on earth with course

Yeah it is a sunny day now

you can see endless diamond stars

shining through in day light in snow

The sky with all its stars now behold

can be seen on earth in joy in burst

The Men

Each man

Is a man onto itself

And a man outside of himself

And a man

Who does not listen

To that man

Who is outside of himself

For advise and recommendation

In the waterless barren desert of creativity

Is doomed to rot under sun

And then be buried alive

In the sand storm

As the fresh food supply

For the scorpions

Meal Time: the King Arthur's Round Table

A seat

Was so conspicuously

Set among all the other seats in arrangement

With distinct recognition in enchantment

Guests came in ...

More guests came in ...

No one went to sit on it

Despite the congestion

And smallness of room

I went to the host

And asked her in whisper...

I am a stranger here

and don't understand

Why no one goes to set on that vacant seat

She said quietly in a gentle voice...

"That who sits on that seat"

"His spirit will abandon him upon contact"

Upon hearing the answer

I thanked God

for not going to sit on that seat

on my own without knowing its horrific consequences

Rain the Drummer, Window the flutist...

The rain is pouring

Make music continuously

On the roof and from the gutter

Yes this is the sound of home

And this sound becomes ever more homey

As the rain keeps pouring for days

There ...

Learn to take care of your roof & gutter on time

To enjoy this primordial music non- stop

That touches your soul closer than

Your own bones

Without being interrupted by

Roof leaking and gutter overflowing

Those two untimely annoyances

Interfering with your music time relaxation

O

Human mind

Is made of

So many fine and finer path ways

Which allow for

Human sublime communication's

In form of delicate art forms

And what not

But there are visions and ideas

So sublime and so delicate

Beyond any human mind's reach for processing

No matter how delicate

The internal structure is woven & crafted

In order to sharing them

With the outside world

Communicably

Be Happy Now...

While alive

Don't

Worry

Too much

About where

You will be buried

After you die

For we all

Live a global village

And in this tiny village

No matter where you buried

You will be so close without a doubt

To your next kin village fellow human being

Even if your body

Is turned into

Dust and powder

Scattered around...

Just Don't Worry!

Never Learn

He

has

climbed

the tallest seven mountains in the world

All the way to the top

yet upon his return

He is still expected to listen and obey those

who in their attempt

have failed to climb

even a smallest hill

in the vicinity

why?

As an acknowledgement that

He has not yet conquered

The tallest mountain ever

The summit of Mt. Heart in victory

To warrant him

The firing squad

To be used against

The disobedient

Gate of Aging Revealed

Transition

From youth

To elderly

Takes place

Through

A fine tunnel

That tunnel

Is nothing

But your own hair line

As it changes color

From what it used to be

To the gray one

To convince you

En route your vision that

It is time

To let the old person

Come inside

To reside in your soul

Instead of blocking it all out

At your door steps swiftly

In The Moment

Social revolution

Is like

An anticipated

Spontaneous

Hot sex

Out of blue

That has lasted

Only for a short intense while

But with bitter unfamiliar consequences

To face with

With no end in sight

It has happened before

It will happen again

And we will again regret it

That's for sure

We will never learn

I guarantee it

When Birds Stop Singing

There were

Six electric cables

Going over my head

And the pagans that you could count them easily

Were sitting in there

The birds kept coming and going

Over my head

Each time a new music note

Was written by pagans on cables over there

The string orchestra went for hours

Created by birds could be overheard

What was the title of their music?

Yes, it was about being polite & courteous

when you are before your dad

Get Me Out of Here~

When

Man's life

Is safe and secure

Greed and envy

Rip through his soul

To push him to acquire

More wealth and greater properties

But when his life in an imminent danger

He is willing to give up everything

Including his underwear

To save his life

This only says

Man's psychic make up

Is made of two extreme and opposite poles of proclivities

And with no happy medium in between

Mercy in Hot Hell...

Put

the lobster

with head first

inside the boiling water

to mammon's his pain and suffering

during the cooking...

And the lobster

gradually change color

From a pale brownish

To a vivid lovely live color

Somewhere between shiny red and orange

What is the subliminal message

Relayed by the Lobster in the boiling water?

Oh the Holy Lord...

Make the boiling and fairy hell fire ever hot and hotter!

Long & Extended Shower

Dust off your room

Polish you mirror

Vic cu mm the carpet

Move the furniture around

To clean the settled spider web

Hiding there as permanent resident

Shine the windows

Change the mattress and pillow cover

With fresh one

Sanitize the surrounding with spray

Let the fresh air blow in

When all is done

You feel as if

You have been baptized freshly clean

In bath tub for hours

Insulated from all the sins around you

There...

The more cleaning & cleansing you do in details

the more sinless you become

Become Water...

Man

By nature

striving with teeth and nail

to go up and climb up more

in the social pyramid of society

yet hardly noticing the water lesson

that constantly descends and descends more

until it reaches the magnificent ocean

some even go way down deeper

to make the underground water reservoir

in the barren desert

For the passing caravan

The river in all dancing

The river in all bouncing

The river in all twisting

The river in all curving

The river in all flip flapping

Always heading down

Rolling...

Life Stages

Man in life

Goes through a series of life stages

Just in the same manner

The caterpillar

Passes through several stages

Until it becomes butterfly

Ready to lay legs

Thus each stage grows into a

Comfortable cozy cocoon one

Before moving into the next

And those men who hesitate

To leave the cocoon on time

By digging a hole in it for escape

Are doomed to be burned alive

In hot boiling water from beyond

Rendering his life mission unaccomplished

Unable to ascend to his next life stage

You have got way comfortable?

This is a warning sign my friend!

Get out at once!

Ocean Mill: Humbling the Rocks

Large rocks...

Smaller rocks...

Rounded stones...

Smaller stones...

Petite marbles...

Now sands ...

As smooth as Chinese silk

But they are all

The procession of

Large to smaller to finer ones in parade

Right before yours eyes

In the grinding machinery of ocean

mill

That has taken the time of eternity

To perform the task

In split second in condensation

For your viewing

Roots of autumn

The season of fall

Has stripped the tall stark trees

From all their leaves

Turning it into a complete naked one

Now after the undressing

The tree looks like

And inverted one in upsetting

With all the underground roots exposed

But this time facing the heaven

With head got stuck in the dark underworld

In complete invisibility

Stone Intelligentsia

Nothing

Bugs

an accomplished

Famous pride intellectual

than to take him

to the graveyard

showing him

His final destiny

with all the books

He has written piled up under his arms

and the medallions

He has been decorated with

now put in the safe lock box

Bed Time Praying: 08

Now

That

I am

Entering

Into the new world of sleep

For several hours

Let me have good dreams

Instead of bad ones

Like a drunken man

Who wish to have an all night joy partying

When his world has been transformed suddenly

From the solid

To that of vapor one without boundary

Musical Improvisation for the Largest Assembled Orchestra

Each leaf

On the tree

Is a string

Is a keyboard

And when the wind blows into the trees

In twist and curve and in rattle

It will make music

With zillions and trillions of leaf notes

All played out in the vast forest platform

Now the autumn has arrived

And the wind has no choice but to improvise

By using trees' trunk and remaining fine and finer branches

As string tool for the music to play

Before the inhabitants of earth

Joy! And Only Joy! Period!

This moon

How many grand human gathering has witnessed

This moon

How many long wars has observed being waged amongst men

This moon

How many human catastrophes on earth has gazed at

This moon

How many prophets & preachers has seen who have come and gone

Surely this moon

Has witnessed quite a lot

Despite his youth and his inexperience

And despite the old age experienced human inhibition on earth

Therefore let's have a round of applause

For this novice moon

Before we get back to our own tiresome &

Everlasting & grown up business of society

Still

It

Is

Time

Now

To

Let

God

Reign

Do

You

Know

What

I

Am

Speaking of

or

You

Don't

Still

I

So
Far
I have not
Seen a leaf
In my whole life
Without full symmetry
Except when some of them
Have here and there a hole
On their thin and fragile 'n delicate bodies
When in season of autumn
Began diving downward
In dance for earth
To utter out loud:
The Perfection
In absolute
At the end
Belongs
To thy
God
O
N
L
Y
A
N
D
O
N
L
Y

Oh Wind Blow Me Away Farther

It

is autumn

and leaves

Separating from mother tree

in death dance

to fly away as far as they can

from their mother

before landing

to declare their freedom

and distance from crowd & congestion

we are all dying for freedom!

Note on the spuramacy of flowers

Almost all fruit tree

In spring time

First their blossoms explode in perfurme

Then the leaves later on follow in burst

To follow the leader for help

For his promises of

Juicy and sweat heart darling "shaftalo"

in summer and early fall

But for fruitless flowers

It appears the other way around is the rule

But why and what is secret?

Or no secret at all

If flowers are only

The soft and refined forms of leaves par excellence

Transformation: The Heavenly Birds

I have hung

A bird feeder

Outside of my room

And intermittently

Here comes this and that bird in boom

During their comfortable feast

On the bird feeder out in Rome

I watch them with my binoculars

While sitting comfortable in my own dome

Now the birds are eating from the bird feeder

Right inside my room

As if their bodies have been transformed into light

to cross so easy the glass window come to my room

Oh the birds are all in my room

Without mess and germs or droppings

While singing and eating free all in my room

Dexterity: **Toward a Flexible World**

Left hand is the eastern hemisphere

The right hand the western one

I gently bring these two half world near each other

Until each finger tip touches its corresponding counterpart

Now I can see the entire rounded planet earth

Formed from my ten fingers

With five windows air burned

Corresponding to five continents exist in earth

Corresponding to five oceans of earth

To make this rounded fingers planet earth complete

Bend the fingers inward and outward

At their point of convergence a bit

Now you see five windows of love opened up on earth

Each after the image of man's heart

The rounded flexible earth

Like the man's beating heart

Body Dimension

I

Am

Body

Do not cross me

For then be one without food

I

Am

Wine

Do not cross me

For you then be one

Without drink and water

Do not cross me...

Give the Outside World a Chance to Speak

Your

Brain

May work

Like a car ingénue

Without interruption

In constant creation of new idea

But it would be unwise

If you don't turn it all off for a while

To let the outside world

Begins to pour its own idea & signs

Into your head

Like a waterfall

Joining the ocean in an astounding sound with a new message

"Fight Kais"

Yes

With only several gallons of water

Along with a hidden water pump

Coupled with all its well camouflaged tubes

You can make a waterfall

That can make soothing sound until eternity

As long as

You can pay the electric bill

With leak free foundation

You want to see a more fancy one

Then let's go Los Vegas

To see Bella lo spectacular water show

When time comes for family vacation

After some hard work done accomplished

Ocean Cow

The ocean

Has brought

Tons of sea weeds and other greenery

On the shore

And then let it all rot and break down

Outside of the sea under the blazing sun

When the time is ready for full digestion

To ocean takes back the regurgitated greenery

Back in to his stomach from the shore to his mouth

Surely the ocean is the cow

Chewing her food twice

Once in hurry

Second in slow motion and gentle

Laying down in comfort under sun

And then right back to his deeper belly

From his shore mouth

Submerged Human Civilization

Most American homes' exterior

Is covered from head to toe

By layers of shingles

Row after row

Just like the fish scales

Not just to protect the body of house

From the beating of sun rays and rain storm

But to remind everyone that

The Atlantic civilization inside the ocean

unlike the popular belief

Is safe and sound and well

With indisputable evidence of

School of fish in standstill

Scattered...

In diverse form of neighborhoods

Bow to Me

Loneliness

Isolation

Defining silence

Frozen in time in standstill

Indeed is a king itself

Standing before you

asking you for submission

You must then

Slaughter this demon king

with the fire of your will power

to regain your freedom in victory

Once Upon a time

Each written line

Is a string in the book

And when you begin to read it

You're in fact

Playing it with the string in the book

Start listening to string music

With headphone one on alone

Even if you are in the middle of crowd

Unless you play this string music

Outlaid for kids at their bed time

Until they fall sleep in melody in rhyme

Connection! Connection! Connection!

A cute

Fluffy

Cuddling

Lamb

And a full grown up male lion

Has fallen

In love with

This bomb

Now come on and see

With the lion protection

What kind of sermon and admonishment

Is delivered before

A pack of hungry wolves

By this adorable lamb

Hours of lectures

With absolute confidence

Being given to the multitude

In Baum!

Marriage of Day & Night

The barren 'n naked bushes and trees

Now have put on a new cloth

In the winter cold

Yes thin layers of transparent crystal

Covering their bodies throughout

On one hand, they appear in their new attire

As sparkling grand and massive chandelier

With moon as its center lamp

In radiance in all directions at night

Hanging from the ground instead of ceiling in suspense

And on the other hand

In day light under clean blue sky with vibrant sun

Appears as the grand diamond bazaar

Where each shop is showing off

Their best shining diamonds

From behind the glass windows

In all sizes and varieties in abundance

What is the occasion?

Yes it is the wedding time between day and night

with an endless exchange of star light diamonds

amongst the participants all willing to pay hefty prices

Running through the colors...

Flowers...

Come in an endless variety

And in an endless perfusion of colors

But seeing is deceiving

For they are the workers of paradise

To help man on earth

To document the invisible spirit

Vividly and visibly for himself

When suddenly a single flower

Catches man's eyes with such force & gravity

With its color

To help him experience the spirit itself in awe

After all days of hard work experienced in full

Tree

Is that emperor
who has not forgotten
His dark empire that must grow
in the rooted underworld
when ascending to the heaven
to expand his empire to embrace the light
O Tree you are indeed the king!
The king of both worlds
And that who mishandles you
Will have the last name of "Treason"
For his offspring's
Messiah was crucified on your body
When he used his saw and hammer and nail from a bit of a wrong angle
How many birds have you let them nest on your soul
How long of a shadow you cast
For the comfort of mankind in the heat of summer
How many lovers made love under your blossom
How many lush green fruits you brought to this world
Sweeter and sexier than the juicy engorged lips of woman
How many more son emperors you generated from within
To be sacrificed for the comfort of man to build his shelters
And how many gallons of pure oxygen you generated for the lungs man
Oh even your dead body is the source of life in warmth in fire
But o you tree know one thing for sure
There is only one nation on the face of earth
Who has respected your soul better all the other ones

Canada!

For in this nation
When one tree
Is chopped down
automatically
A baby is put
Right back
In the soil
to remember
Its humanity
En route eternity

125

Roots of Blossom Leaves

Leaf

Blossom

Flower

Fruitw

Honey Bees

Bumble bees

The falling seeds in fall

They are all huddled together as one

In a tiny soft pillow like arrow

On various parts of tree branches in spring

Before they explode in full in sequence

Each going in separate direction

To change their destiny

Just like the womb of mother

Within it

There is so much untold mystery

Blindfolded

What

An architect a bird is

For once the couple

Arrange some straws together tightly knit

On the top of a tall tree

They know for certain that

Nothing can come to their nest

To snatch their babies away

Even when the deep darkness of night

Has carpeted their nest

In an absolute blindfolding

In the silence of forest

Even when the crickets

Have stopped singing

Rising State of Bird hood

With the current state of deforestation

The birds of all variety & kind

Must learn to set aside

Their superficial differences

To arrive at the state of their bird hood consciousness

In order to put their nests

In closer and closer proximity

Without too much squabbling over lack of space

Until the last tree

Vanishes from the face of the earth

Then they begin to fight each other again

Now imagine the magnificent cardinal

Living in few inches apart

From the noisy crow as he nourishes his babies

This is what we call tolerance

If you did not know its true meaning

In the age of global warming

Emperor's Execution Order Is Complete Now

In late September

Still all leaves

Fully intact on trees

The pouring rain

Along with strong wind

In several continuous days in row

Has carpeted the land with live green leaves

Reminding the world that

Natural cause of death

is only one kind

among all the other causes of death

yes my friends

the season of "falls"

Is a four season reality

even when there is no leaves on trees

that one can speak of

Pristine

I live in a village

Those streets have no name

The passing cars have no plate number

The houses are devoiced of number identity

When people want to find your address

They look into the signals being given off

In the written calligraphy of frosting

On branches of trees in winter

In awesome shapes of leaves as they in star constellation on earth

Tell you what street you should not go into

In awakening sounds of birds as they come to fly from one tree to the next

To give you a tentative map that must be completed

By your own sense of imaginative improvisation

And at the end when you get to me in this village

You must have been so intoxicated by such musical road finding in

ecstasy

That only to find you on my door step unconscious

For the overdose

One day in Ramadan...

They asked me to go on fasting
when the month of Ramadan arrived
I obliged!
I got up way early before the dawn
Ate some food and drank some tea and water
From there on I refrained from eating and smoking and drinking altogether
What I was allowed to do only was to breathe
Even full submergence in the water was prohibited
I endured the deprivation completely and fully
From the dawn all the way to some late minutes after the sunset
And then began to eat
My face first busted and engorged into redness
From the sudden infusion of energy
As if I had finished up the whole bottle of wine in one sitting
The joy of eating was so spectacular and awesome
So much so that I had never experienced
Any thing like it in my entire life
From that burst of energy
I have grown up in faith to love food and respect food
and never ever go on fasting even for one more day
Except for medical testing that comes
in the early morning after the sun rise
Thus my attachment to food
remains inseparable with no interruption
until I slide gently into my grave site
if I can ever afford paying for the expenses

Then they said you are allowed to eat

Fifth Script: The Table Rose

There are five kinds of scripts in the entire world

The first script is

Both the writer and reader understand it

The second script is

When only the writer understands it and not the reader

The third script is

When the reader understands it but not the writer

The fourth script is

When neither writer nor the reader understand it

The fifth script is

When no script is written at all

For the world at large itself is illiterate par excellent

I'm reigning now

All

The ills

Of our time

At the end

Rooted in one factor only

• The population growth—

To have a future for mankind

Then one child per family please

With automatic vasectomy for the man

Upon the birth of first child

For each and every family

Around the globe

As precondition for the release of baby

From the hospital

Impending Famine:
The Dictatorship of Hot & Cold Fusion

I

Am

Not

Against kissing

At all

But when it comes to choose

Between food and hot kissers

Man's lips must choose hot food

No more discussion on this matter!

Okay?

The end of argument!

Taste of Meal after Work

Sun!

Is my running mate

Together we run on mirror like flat beach platform

Ocean!

Is my enthusiastic audience in constant standing ovation

with roaring crushing waves

the blue sky!

Is my hat

Keeping me safe

from the harmful sun rays from above

did I miss any thing here?

O yes

when the running is over

I will be in the exotic restaurant

Eating in variety

as if I am a welcome quest in paradise

after a day long hard work running...

Tall Evidence

Fang of hunger

It was excruciatingly painful

And my stomach kept sending

Strong signals after signals with no interruption

To my brain

That it must do something right now and right this minute

I looked at my stomach from outside

For check and balance for accuracy

I found it full and pretty much swollen

And I told myself: What a lie

With the tall stack evidence against its claim visible

How on earth it possibly have a winning case

In the court of mind and body and health

In battle for supremacy

The Quiet Night

The camp fire in dance

With sparkles in explosion in bang

The clean sky full of winking stars

Alone with my guitar

Playing a cool melody outside of my tent with heart

Sipping whiskey to witness the night

The coffee is gently brewing in the pot

In the nearby pristine lake

I hear the sudden splash of fish

Jumping up and down under the moon light

This is my only refuge

Away and from the barbarism of man

In their so called civilized collectively

I play guitar alone

Until I fall asleep in my tent...

In Praise of Honor

Thanks

God

For

Making death inevitable destiny for man

so he can learn to begin to live

in dignity

in honor

in grace

the three necessary ingredients

for man to rise from the dead

after experiencing the inevitable

Amen!

Dr-If-T-ER

I

Am

A drifter

A free man par excellence

And my freedom

Comes to an end

In cold winter

When I have to huddle together

With bunch of slabs

That they say there are my associates

Slurping the free hot soup

In coning suffocating places

They call it "shelter"

In order to ride out the winter

Until spring comes

To become a free man once again

One thing though is for sure

The police do not like our kind

To flourish on planet earth

Nor their inhabitants

Except during the holiday

When Christmas is around the corner

Control: Separation is separated

The moment

Man gets

Sick or

Becomes

Impaired

Physical or mental

Even minor one

His world begins to become separated

from the world of healthy one

and those who ignore

This wall of reality

Will surely fall in the whirlpool of

Miscommunication in anger

There...

To avoid unnecessary explosion

between these two world

Remember the "Pause" and "Pausing"

Open Door & Fresh Air

The

House

You are living in

Indeed could become

The place where the demon resides

When you keep it all sealed off

To the outside world

As if it exists in separation

And away from the country

There...

An open house

is a house

that demon has no nerve

to stay in there

Even for one second

Head Up: Taking Notice

Geese have made

An arrow head formation

In their flight up in sky

As they fly toward the new destination

All sing songs out loud together

Not to beef up more energy amongst the themselves

During the journey

And not to coordinate the positioning of geese

In the arrow head formation

And certainly not to admonish in loud voice

Those who have fallen a bit behind

But that they sing for man on earth

With loud voice

So he would notice

His majestic heavenly singing sign of king in floatation

Without ever missing that great opportunity by accident

When his head down

Concentrating only on his immediate world affairs

Year Round Blue Lawn

I

Love

Lush green lawn

And obsessed with it

to make sure

there is not a tiny single spot left

to remain barren or bald

Even if it requires patching

Like a poor old lonely man's jacket patching on his elbow

And since this is almost impossible

With the existing means at my disposal

The only refuge I have

To overcome my obsession with full green lawn

Almost on the border line of madness

I to raise my head up see the blue sky

As my light blue lawn

With cloud patches gently moving

To turn it up utterly immaculately dateless

Old Man with Youthful Thoughts

A massive solid rock

sits out in the open ocean

you can see it all easy

it is not too far from the shore

in stands still not in the motion

the yesterday snow has covered up

the top head of rock in full

with sun shine rays in reflection

Looks like an old man

putting on his hairs

Some kind of lotion

And black docks sitting in abundance on the head of old man

They say we are the symbol of young and fresh thoughts

Emanating from the head of old man

Yes! With young and fresh thoughts

the old man rock in sea is still young

Even though he is in standstill without any motion

Wringing

He

May cover

His head for protection

With layers after layers of clothing

Until it becomes turban

But he must beware of

The right foot of

Full grown male elephant

When it comes down upon his head Genteelly

Smashing it

Under its soft heavy force

Like a blown apart water Malone

Endless Blue Sky

I am sitting on a chair

I am tired after so much work but fair

The air conditioner blowing at my hair

With an unusual sound just like jet plane in air

With this exhaustion I feel I am in sky

Falling in sleep with both of my shoes on in pair

Oh this jet plane is going so smooth and so rare

Despite its thunderbolt speed

Chasing sun in orbit day and night in dare

The Earth force jet plane is awesome

Flying in blue sky motionless oh this so rare

Believe it or not in this jet plane

There is garden and lawn and apples and pears trees

Air conditioner blowing in jet plane sound like for more cares

Arrest All the Copy Cats at Once & Now

Beware of

The imitators

For with their wicked craft

They can mimic the original

Far better than the original itself

Thus giving them an upper hand

To throw & dump anything that is original

Right into the whirlpool of stinky waste basket

The way the emitters are expanding the empire

There will be a day on earth in a very near future

The word original

Has been wiped out clear

From man's consciousness and his psyche

Arrest them all at once

And put them in tight painful shackles

Wherever you see them

Unimaginable: The Depth of Bed

I

Had to

Abandon her

For I knew

If I take one more step

To get any closer to her

I would have become glued to her inseparable

Then I would engage myself in

Any imaginable or

Unimaginable

Measures

To make sure for certain

We will be together breath to breath

Heart to heart

At all times

And nothing could ever possibly

Dare

Come between us

Fall of the Dictator

I
Put
A magnifying mirror
In front of my face
In a close up
I see a bit larger image of myself
I enjoy the enlargement quite a lot ...
I distance the mirror from my face a bit more
I see a bit larger image than the previous one
Thus I enjoy it even more
I keep distancing the mirror from myself
So I can increase my joy ever more
Instead I get an unspecified
Confused unreadable image
In fragmentation
Like a drunken man with excess drink
throwing up in convulsion with head down in toilet
I struggle to get myself back after its breakdown in shattering
By furthering the mirror a bit more
But this time
I get an inverted and quite smaller degraded image of
My ordinary self
Like a hated dictator that
Has been belittled by the masses in a revolution
And then being dragged in street in utter humiliation

Modern Homeless

When

Man's roof

Is leaking

And can't fix it

For lack of money or otherwise

His next option

Is to move to his new residence

Which is his car

Without complaining

About the lack of space

If he wish not to get his cloth wet

In the next storm rain

Love on the Wheelchair

A man

Who has been

Put on the wheelchair

Due to his bodily injury

Must take advantage of

His uplifted heavenly position

Like Christ on the cross

So that he would not ever again

Get too involved

In the bloody

Hateful

Dirty

Bitter

Affairs of man on earth

If not then

Everyone would come and say

See ...

He deserves the current condition of his suffering

Deep Memory

I have hung

A long bird feeder onto the tree

Full of seeds

In cold winter with snow covering the surface of earth

All sorts of starving birds come to eat

From the hanging heaven with the seeds

Even with the squirrel proof bird feeders

You see the squirrel comes in suspense in insertion

To eat from it like having orgy in licks

Who is not coming to eat from this suspended heaven in air?

The crow... yes the crow

And when you beam it in dilapidated communication for an answer

The bird replies:

You have no idea what it tastes

When you nibble the baby birds delicacy

Snatched right out from their nest

Hot and fresh in spring in feast

Baby I can wait for that taste delicacy

Throughout the winter

Even if it means to starve when all have feast

Thief Kings

Cheap sun glasses

Are left inside the shop

Free and easily accessible to public

For exam and possible purchase

But the moment

They become expensive with famous label

They are put behind the window in safe lock box

This only says

Man by nature has a tendency to become a thief

And at any moment

He could be tempted to snatch the valuable

To improve his chances for a better life

Even if he comes from a higher moral ground

As High as of a King

Now let's move to the topic of diamonds

French Revolution: Equality, Justice, Liberty

I hardly

Know a person

Who has not bought or purchased

Public lottery tickets

To get a chance

To win a large sum of money at once

This says everyone wishes to be wealthy

Yet paradoxically there is such an accusation & resentment

Amongst the poor toward the rich people

Who also buy the same ticket to become even wealthier

Just like the famous proverbial Persian cat

Who is unable to reach that fresh tender meat?

Says in a disgruntled gesture

"pew… that meat stinks …not eatable"

The Rethinking of the "Atom"

Hummingbird

In sky

flying

yet in stand still

As if it is frozen in time

by a photographer

in his best snap shot

For an award winning photo competition

Beyond Sermon: In Praise of Vacuum

Oh

She cleans

The room

Bring all the scattered junkies

Into the union

All in one basket in friendship

Ready for collective journey for another destiny

O vacuum!

You not only clean up the room crystal clean and away from the debris

But also in your ever omnipresent mighty sucking

You eject out the bad spirit

That is hanging out all over the room

In utter invisibility

O you vacuum

All the praise goes to you

For you both cleanse the body and spirit all at once

Amen!

Choose the High Ground

Words

Are sturdy trap

Use

This

Trap

Toward

Your own advantages

Your own progress

Without being imprisoned by it

To do it

Read the sentence

Knowing there is more to read

With no end in sight

Bonding

Each page

Is a leaf

If all pages

Are bonded together as book

With a nice front and back cover

Now you have tree

Have you had a good luck

With the book sale?

Then you are looking not at the tree but at the forest

First thing first

My children were borned

Thus I became father

They married and had children

I still remained as their father

My children's children married and had children

I continued to remain my their father

They came to me and they said

When are you going to become grand father

My response was put into only one word: never!

They said how come?

I replied because I am my father's son

Thirty Plus

You are right

When I was a kid

And bumped into someone

Whom I knew he was forty

I would be shaken to the very core in fear

By his massive age discrepancy

Knowing for sure

I am near a very strong and mature man

Towering over my head like a giant

Who could snap in anger in any second without notice

To smash me under his heavy iron long feet

I am now nearly 60 year old

and still frightened by

the greatness & horror and vastness of forty plus something

Stay Beautiful

To each story

To each claim

There are two sides

Therefore learn to stay

Fit and thin and sharp and agile

Like a tender leaf money

In order to be able

To see the two sides of

The same coin as a whole in fullness

Before rushing to the court

With all your documents at hand

Like a tall stack of bonded money

Pointing to your righteousness

To settle account in your favor

Before the judge

Fight Over Distinction & Honor

In autumn

each leaf

Separates itself

from the mother tree

and comes down

not like any other leaf

in its own unique trajectory

dancing...

Swirling...

Falling...

Flip flopping

rotating...

Diving...

Rising...

Flying...

Like a unique finger print of a

New born child

to announce to the world that:

"I am now a leaf never seen before on earth"

Seagull the Fluffy Rock

Seagulls fly in the air
Together or alone gliding in the air
Seagulls playing in the air

diving from air to sea to make a catch
fighting each other in mid air
to snatch each ocher's catch.

In windy stormy day
they stay stand still in the air.

After their meal for digestion
they sit swollen relaxing
Contemplating in the pair

they do it all these things
in all four seasons without a gang
as if they are all identical with or without the rank.

Yes the bird seagull is the rock itself
Considers the distinction between all four seasons
Just another man's baseless invention
When he cannot live by his skin alone
With or without the sang.

Not a Laughing Matter

In Autumn

Trees are in competition

With one another

To shed their leaves

As generous and as philanthropic as possible

To make sure

Their chance for resurrection

In the after life

Is not denied

Believe it or not

Some go so far

To become fully naked

Before public eyes

Without the slightest shame

You thought it was that easy? Think Again

A great artist

Must lead a life in isolation

A sort of pariah and untouchable

The creature of rejection

Beyond understanding and comprehension

The product of distance

So when his work is finished

Later on can be appreciated by masses

But better posthumously

So his "crime" and his germ of innovation

Leaves the masses untouched and unharmed

By preventing the break out

Of a possible social epidemic

Like a run away dinosaur in Jurassic Park now in rampage

Greed Is Good: Always More Room Left to Eat

Leaves of Bread

Are left unattended

as the starving people

devouring the leaves of money

in the lifeless barren desert of greed

with no hope in sight

if they ever get fed

to leave this table

in contentment

Humanity of Deep Wound

Whispering wind

Dancing leaves

Swirling falling tree branch

Dying colorful flowers

Disappearance of bird songs once played in orchestra

The undressing of trees near fool nakedness

Smell of rotten leaves

The sound of crushing leaves under man feet

Together define

The humanity of autumn

Old Shingles

Here it comes

He says drink it

This is a glass of fine wine

I said what is in it

He said nothing

But keep you drunken for all time

I asked with only one glass of it?

He said absolutely affirmatively yes

So I sat on the chair

And drank the permanent glass of wine

First the wind began to blow suddenly

Moving trees with leaves in late spring in agitation

So I could hear their music orchestra never heard before

I Alta on the chair watching time unfolding

Saw my house that I was before me

Crumbling ...

Slowly...

Gently

Until I found myself warped in wrapped rags homeless

With wild cats and dogs and other derelicts as companions

yet still happy and drunken as if living in paradise

Things You Never Forget

Instead of

Spoon feeding me

with clear cut answer

she gives me an incomplete design...

A tentative map...

Suggestion...

Hints...

Mystical winking...

A thought full pause...

A little sweet smile decorating her eyes...

And when I put together

All the sings and signals together

And find the answer on my own

This time the discovery

Sinks all the way to the bottom of my mind

Like a stone going down straight

To hit and stay at the bottom of ocean

For complete remembering

Yes, this is the way

To remember God during the gardening

In tangible way

Like holding the Conch statue at hand for assurance

When too busy uprooting the weeds

Winterizing Poetry

Autumn has ended

Trees all are naked

Echo of traffic now has a different sound

These are true signs that

We have become winter bound

Spirit of winter demands man

To become all wrapped up

Like trees full of leaves

When the fall had not begun

I search for amazement during the shortening days

I search for amazement during the lengthening nights

I find reading and writing poetry quite fine

There is music in some poems

That fills the winter air vacuum like warm blanket

When all the leaves are all gone

Spirit of Flowers: Let There Be Sun & Water!

The Impatient...

From birth

to death

it has only

one pledge

and one vow

To fulfill

The promise of flowering

without stop

without hiatus

without interruption

and without betrayal

that is

to keep flowering

and to never leave its leaves

without the ornamentation of

Relentless blossoming in abundance

the zero tolerance!

That is what the impatient amounts to...

Falling Perspective: Atom

In autumn

Each leaf

On the tree

Is a king

But since

They do not have

Ties to soil

Like roots

Deep and deeper

They all fall

One after another

On the face of land

As they turn into powder

And then blown away

In metamorphosis

Into so many microscopic species in belittlement

Rest in Peace

Leaves falling

Fragile

Lifeless

Dead

And can be blown away

With the slightest breeze

But I pile them together

And with some sacrifice

The rest are holding together tight in unity

Defying the strongest wind in standstill

While holding their ground

Demanding a respectful burial

Cheating

They have thrown me

Into the woods in blind folded ness

Yet expecting me

To paint the leaves and trees

And all the surrounding

In separate art work canvas

By relying only on

The feeling of smell I get

From the breeze

And on the sound I hear from

The creatures in the vicinity and afar

Therefore with all these limitations

I have no choice

But to cheat

That is to stick out my tongue

To taste the forest in its totality

If all the touching of surrounding

Can't give me clues as to what is it that

I am supposed to see

For my art work

King on the Throne

Leaves

One

After

Another

are pushed off the branches

descending ...

And as they in dance

Fall gently

Touch earth

Realize for the first time

their source of their identity

is way vast beyond their mother ...

Thanks to mother tree

for her austere identity education

Moving to My Beverly Hills Mansion

How many times we have seen sun set and sun rise

How many times we have seen all the phases of moon

How many times we have witnessed

The coming and going of the four seasons

And the roaring of blue ocean

How many times we have observed clouds moving in blue sky

Making shapes after shapes

How many times we have noticed and heard the pouring rains

How many times we have zoomed on leaves dancing falling in fall

How many times we have seen stars at night with might

How many times we have entered and left the same house

How many times we have exchanged the same hello & how are you

How many times we traveled into night until day

Yet despite all these repetitions

We wish to see them again without novelty

Experience: Hold on to It for a Little Longer

When the music is great

You want to hear it louder

When the fabric is silky soft

You want to touch it longer

When the scenery is beautiful

You want to get to it closer

When the smell is awesome

You want to inhale it deeper

But when the food is great and delicious

Please don't gobble it all up in rush

For you then miss the life time experience

I know it I know it

On the last item

You need constant reminders

My Beloved Binocular

In early spring

A red cardinal

Was singing

In awesome strong voice

To attract a lover

To build a nest to form a family

And no matter how far

He flew away from one branch of this tree

To the next and that distant tree

I could feel & see

He is till singing in strong voice

While sitting on the tip of my fingers

In close up

Thanks to my super strong binocular at once!

But don't let Cardinal know about this

for he might decide signing next time

in camouflage behind the leaves

Laughing Apple Tree in autumn

Leaf to me is the smile and laugh

Trees put them on

To say the time is getting friendly with a better half

Now the cold weather has come about

And trees begin one after another

To shed playing as well as their belly laugh

But my apple tree keeps on its belly laugh

As if it is an evergreen lover for silly half

And I tell myself with all these apple laughing

No wonder the apple tree perfumed blossom in spring

Is the best and better half

Exhausted Champions

Athletics often use

The upper echelon of their will power apparatus

To get their "Physique" moving in agility with strength

Not knowing though that to leave

The rest of their will power

apparatus idle for long

They may risk become paralyzed

And then scorned upon for laziness

When it comes to do some quick moves and chores

Around the house to do some trivial low energy work

Those champs who can crawl out of

This death lower chamber apparatus toward some activities

Will earn my most earnest respect with no reservation

Resisting Leaves

Fall ...

Leaves...

They are pushed off by mother tree

They are deprived from food

In complete disconnection

They have gotten heavier from constant rain

And still heavier

By constant blowing wind around them

Yet despite all the odds

Some of the leaves holding on tight to their mother

Refusing to accept the inevitable

As they see their comrades

One after another in great numbers

Breaking ranks right before their eyes in a nose dive downfall

Signals

It is late December but instead of cold

I heard singing birds chirping ready to mate

I witnessed the shooting of rose leaves in utter beauty

I felt the warm of sun rays burning into my skin

Trying to get in touch with my cheek bone

I felt excess sweating in the normal clothing I wear in winter

As if I put them on right after playing a great active soccer game

I ignored them all!

Until I bumped into patches of full grown blue purple pansies

Now I am asking you

Should I take personal responsibility for global warming

by dry cleaning much of my cloths instead of buying them brand new?

Or simply ignore this one as well

By saying... this is my way...

And I am not going to compromise my life style even for one bit

For I love brand new stuff for ever!

New Record: Happy 200th Birthday Grand Pa

Despite

All the deforestation

Still whenever man sees

A stark old tree

With several hundred years of age

Recorded in concentric circles

Inside its belly

He treats the tree with awe, revere and astonishment

But when it comes to man

By the time he hits 90's

Everyone more or less

Expects his to die

For one's own comfort

Hundredth birthday?

Hurry at once to bring me the chain saw

Live Spirit

An Immigrant

Has come to settle

In another country

And with so many years passed

He has managed to prepare for himself

A relatively modern and clean place

That one can call it home

But the immigrant

Is nostalgic still

Longing for his own native home

Feeling his home

Is empty devoid of fire, life, and living spirit

As if living in planet moon

Abandoned and alone

He uses his mind and install a large mirror

Now from this vintage point large window

He call see a duplicate of his residence

In his own home native country

Yet imbued with life and spirit

Typical of the conditions present in planet earth

In Memory of Kurdistan

I have hung

Several wind chimes

With different vibration sound and intensity

From a tree in my backyard

And when in a sunny day

Wind blows into them

I sit on a flat chair relaxing and listening

Thinking I am a Shepard

Taking a break during work

In the vast pristine infinite golden Kurdistan pasture

While my sheep and goats

Gently moving in slow motion in vicinity around me

So I can hear from their sounding bells

The full orchestral bell symphonic

Stressing this primordial truth that

The future and survival of mankind as species

Can only be guaranteed

In small and self sustaining luxurious villages

Hand Picked Heavenly Earth

The tree leaves in autumn

Have all fallen on earth

Yet they're all asking

To be uplifted back in heaven not earth

As each show off

The mark of its heavenly stars in pierce with force

And I search and search until

I pick up that leaf maple large and embolden

It's being set ablaze

In deep burgundy

For heaven and for new earth

It's astounding

All over

There are stars

On this leaf in fire in burst

I Am Beautiful & Strong

Barely larger than an inch

yes that small!

But to attract his lover in spring

one can hear his singing courtship

On the top of tree

more than half a mile away

yes that far!

Just imagine

if this tiny bird

was about the size of a grown up crow

what powerful music one could hear

in forest

perhaps as far as the crow

could fly

from one end of the forest

to the other

Kurdistan

In late after noon

When the sheep return home

From their long day journey

They leave a rising dust behind

And bring an orchestra of bell music in

When they enter into the muddy houses

Filled with

sounds

Activities

Hassle and Bustle

Anticipation for fresh milk

Etc.

And there is not a single child found in the village

that has not yet been awakened

to this sound effervescence of life in movements

during and after the sunset

Gap

Oh good old days

When a new idea came to my mind

I could hold on to it

For more than a day

Before turn and mold it

Into a beautiful musical poetic prose

With awesome impact

In vibration of resonance

But look at me now

Between receiving the idea

And running to find a pen to write it down

I find myself forgetting

What was that?

I was about to compose

However, I hope one of these days

It will hit me in the head once again

As a reminder

Not as a falling brick

But as a soft gentle touching leaf

Falling in autumn over my hairs

Wheel of Fortune: Will It Be May Again?

Life

Is like a merry-go-around

You hop on it in a season

That could be spring, winter, summer, or fall

And then begin to see

Season after season before your eyes

In rotation

Without boredom despite repeat and repetition

Until it stops in a season

That may or may not

Correspond to the season of your entry

Reza Shah of Persia

Oak leaves

All fall down

In autumn

Except those

That have not gone high up

Thus defying the law of nature

The

Rise

And

Fall

Of

Leaf

Lust for Oxygenation

In each and every room in the house

Resides a spirit, a feeling

Out there is yet another one in the yard

Until you leave the house entirely for the public domain

Now you experience the final Spirit, the spirit of all

With capital "S" to emphasize its all encompassiveness

The roaring seas and the blooming leaves

All at work as servers & servants to the spirits

Whether in or out or inside out

The Night Journey

Wind blows

Into the light body of

A fallen brownish leaf

Forcing it running for a while on its edge wheel

On a flat yesterday snow in a sunny day

Leaving behind foot prints after foot prints

Saying outbound:

Traveling without a trace

Is only a figment of imagination?

No matter how light one can get

Falling without a fall

My happy apple tree

That I planted on the top of a giant rock

When it was a baby

Has grown up in maturity into two separate directions

Upward and downward

One to heaven

The other to earth

With apples dangling down

From all its branches

Thus, those branches

Touching the earth

Newton won't hear a thing from it

For apples are already

Attached to the earth

As well as to the heaven

Both at the same time

Did you know that

Half of this rare tree was cut off by a hurricane

When its western side wasn't greatly appreciated for some unknown

reason?

Golden Poinsettia

An amazing plant

A source for reverie

Her heart shaped leaves

Transforming themselves

From deep austere green

Into bright light vivid burgundy

In illumination

Right before your eyes

From one extreme of color

To another

How one can explain

This mystery of transformation without a trace

Without witnessing the flow of milk

Running in her vain in abundance

Ready for suckling

"Taste of fall"

Aluminum foil

Wrapped all around few potatoes

Together in solidarity

Thrown into the hot charcoals fire

Out in the open inside the grill

As they all covered by the

Dry leaves of autumn

Burning in smoke

In less than twenty minutes

You for the first time

Taste the authentic uncompromising season of fall

As you season the opened up roasted potatoes

With salt, pepper and sweet butter…dissolving

Before spooning it out

Into the all watery mouth of yourself &

The enthusiast children in anticipation

Sweet Cherries

For Ned & the Family

Large, white yellowish, juicy cherry

So expensive to buy it in large amount

Instead I settle for couple of dozens

Now what is left of it?

Is white rounded seeds

I quickly burry planting them in the soil

And like Buddha Squatting close to them in meditation

Visualizing the growth of seeds to a starter

Then to transplantation in suitable spot

Then the leaves

Then the blossom, the bees, the perfume

Now the fruits in plenty for all to eat

And in the midst of devouring the cherries

My lover says I wish they were a little sweeter

Surrender

My relatives, I love no more

The neighbors, I care less

People in the town, you have to be kidding

The colleagues at work place, it only makes me to throw up

Instead, I love the gentle sea waves

Coming ashore to wash my bare feet in humility

Instead, the movement of wind on leaves

To make music in gentle whisper

Instead, the shining diamond dew in absolute transparency

Ornamenting the roses up until late morning

Instead, the color of rain bow in vast sky

After the end of a sudden rain in summer

And when my family, my neighbors

My town people, my colleagues

Begin to take note of such signs in their behavior

Then I begin to like them too

But only bit by bit

Like the drippings of icicle under warm sun in winter

Where each drop worth's a world

Use the Mirror in Moderation

Muslims who go on pilgrimage journey

are strictly forbidden

to look at themselves

in the mirror

among the host of other things

including the sexual intercourse

but why?

Well...perhaps the mirror lies

for it can not accurately

Show for fact

how old one's soul is

for the mirror only scratches the surface of man's skin

Without ever delving deeper into his spirit

to reflect his true longevity

But of course

The best of all mirrors is

When we see yourself

In the collective looking glass eyes of others

As to how they perceive us

Entrapped Moisture

I planted the first tree

The second, the third,

Now I sit back and look at them

With their intense competition for position and place

Pushing their roots ever deeper into the soil for survival

And somehow this push makes them all grow faster

Oh I love the damp moist that gets caught between the spread out

Leaves

Reminding me that I have succeeded to make forest

Right in my back yard

You may call me Mr. Squirrel

But the one that brings diversity

When planting core and seeds without expectation for return

Oh this entrapped moisture between the leaves

Is so promising in attracting more rain to come

Seen and Not Seen

I am wind

When I blow you see me through leaves

As they move and begin to talk to you

I am wind

You see me when I move the cotton clouds in sky

In their ever changing images for the fun of children

I am wind

You see me when I move the ship

I am wind

When you can't see me for I am many

Wedding Celebration under Acres of Cherry Blossom

Cherries' blossoms are amazing

They shoot out way ahead of the green leaves

Turning the tree

Into a bride from head to toe covered in white garment

And then begin to descend like snow flakes in dance

From the body of cherry blossom bride

Carpeting the earth in white satin snow

Day in and day out for weeks

Under the self confident hot solar rays in rising temperature

Yet they hardly melt

And constantly bees and rare birds

Come touching smelling the brides' mild perfume

Asking where the grooms are hiding

Ambition & Upward Mobility

Leaves

In order to

Change their point of origin

From earth to heaven

They risk

Disconnecting themselves from the tree

To drift in heaven air

Even if it means

Just only for few seconds

Therefore

May we change the name of the season?

From fall to rise

Just only for...

Patent

If after several hard look

You can not spot and locate

The signing bird on the tree

Then by accident you have discovered

A singing tree

Yes, a singing tree

Therefore, immediately go to

The town clerk for report

To patent your discovery

Vagabonds

In my garden

There are crawling plants

They love to climb over

My fruit or ever green trees

And then stand on the top of them

As they suffocate them

To claim victory

With a huge V sign

But hey are not like

Sweet grapes with extending hands

To spread love with their juice

And that is why

I take the pleasure

To snip them right in the mid air during their invasion

In vasectomy sound

With my sharp & petite seizer

To say out loud

My home is not a deserted castle

To be occupied by the vagabonds

Mercy: That's for Sure!

Despite being dead

The yesterday leaves

From the last year slaughter

Still rolling in early spring

In the wind of change

In all possible directions

Announcing to the world that

We might be all dead for one year now

But still we can testify as witness

To the rebirth of our own kind

In utter freshness in beauty

As they spring up in this spring

Right back up again

We did not die in vain!

That's for sure!

Vision of Beneath

A stark tree in early spring

Spreading its naked branches

Over a calm pond in parallel

And with sunshine radiating from pond to the heaven

A light breeze makes the reflection of sun rays on branches

Like a tree decorated

With winking electric light in Christmas time in full

But only if one can see this spring celebration of Christmas

From Beneath

As sun turns into a blazing wood fire flame

From within the shaking pond

Do You Hear the Rhythm?

The

Yesterday

Heavy snow

Gently melting

On the top roof of my house

In a sunny day

Dipped in crystal clean blue sky

The melting snow

Makes lovely music

From the gutter of my house

As if still the blue sky is raining

In a sunny day without stop

Impossible Miracle

My happy apple tree

Has grown up in two separate direction

Upward and downward

One to heaven

The other to earth

With apples dangling down

From all its branches

Thus, those branches

Touching the earth

Newton won't hear a thing from it

When apples fall

For apples are already

Attached to the earth

As well as to apple tree

Icicle: No Limit

This time Icicles

Cover every thin and large branch

In thin transparent wrap

Now tree turn into a massive diamond ring unheard of

With so many cuts in brilliance

And here you see massive diamonds

Shining one after another

Trees after trees in forest

To say out loud

When the diamond shines in a sunny blue sky

There is no limit

To its size

Nor to the number of its cuts

Are You Kidding Me

Expensive drinks

He gently slurps in the bar

Eats delicious expensive meal

in the restaurants

But when it comes to wear clean cut attire

He chooses the worn out shredded cheap clothing

to project a sense of being poor

Like a Taliban's with wrinkled ragged turban

To enhance his claim of righteousness

And anti establishment rebel

Despite tons of great second hand clothing's

Being given out by the effluents

For public usage and distribution

When next time you see these folks

Wearing the clothing of contradiction

Instead of normal exchanging of "how Re you"

Say: Are you Kidding me

Conspirators Exposed

Some great people

Never see how great they have become

To witness their fame and great name

While alive

Their greatness

Will only become all apparent

Sadly only posthumously

What a petty though

All because

They could not find a way

To rip through the snare of belittlement

That they were caught in

By the evil doers

When there is a will

There must be a way

Beethoven's thunder and lightening Rain Storm

Most musicians

Are in the danger of

Losing their hearing ears

To the point of going deaf

All because

The only way they can experience

The Fantastic Glorious Beauty

In pristine authentic way

Is through

Loud and all possible Loudest sound

As if they were all burned blind & illiterate

To experience the loud sounds of greatness

In written musical notes

But one thing is for sure

There will not be a single mouse left

That can survive in such loud sounds

Even if it is hidden inside of

An all insulated sound proof wall

Poor mouse!

Let me cry for it

only if it is a cute Mickey mouse!

Known & Unknown

After they

Brought him down

From the cross

They noticed

A deep wound

On his belly

In addition

To four deep wounds

Made by those tree nails

This made them

Realize that

He was way deeper

And more than

What they thought he was

That is layers

Upon layers and

Upon Layer of

History unexplored

Becoming

In the magic rose garden

There rest a rose bud

With the pointed arrow over its head

And covered layer upon layer by pinkish green guardian

Impenetrable

I come close to open a dialogue with the bud

Asking why it does not open

And the bud says

I am all opened up indeed

And in all conceivable colors

As long as you can imagine me that way

I asked what color you are really in full blown

The bud said I am red but imagine me blue

Glory of the Underworld

I am longing
For an old wine cellar
With humid slippery stair cases
Going down and further down
To reach them
In utter darkness
I love the perfume of old dust
Sitting on the bottles
In patience since antiquity
To me in these emasculate historic grave yards
One can find the bone of my ancestors
Who fought for love?
That must spread for humanity
Beyond border & shallow hastened convention
Oh this humidity in the cellar
Remind me that my
Soul is of the same nature
As my good old grand grand grand... more grand father
Oh I love antiquity!
For in its dust
I find the vapor of freshness air to breathe
In a sunny day one find by old sea
Let me hold one of you in my hand now
To bring you en route the slippery damped stair cases
To the light of surface
To uncork you
To hear your ancient sound of pouring
To share you with friends for few hours
That could last for millennium
With its imprint on one's soul memory
O the glory of you in your underground dress in dust
Is at par with the beauty of sun light after the storm in rain bow

A Reflection on Honor Killing

From day one

You are burned

Treat your close relatives

And later on your spouse and children

As your good friends

So when some of them

Lose their way and go astray in the future

You then only feel a friend has gone

Trying to find a way if possible

To throw a rope for their rescue

Without experience of

Any hard feeling that comes in form of extreme violence

This way you end up

Helping your relatives

In the best possible friendly way

under all possible circumstances

With or without baptism

T Room

I

Put a collection of

Colorful flowers in a jar with water

They shine and glorify the t room

Like a magnificent guest in awesome attire

Visiting me for few days in my home

In less than a week though

The jar spewing out bad odor

Worse than smell of foot soldier toes

Left in boots in month without being exposed

To fresh soap and water, air with force

Indeed! Even flowers without roots

Can later on become source of

Bad odor, demon in curse

Perhaps the only way to save

The rootless wild flowers for long

Is dried them in suspense

Until they become valuable in purse

Mimicking

Squirrels in late October

With the most of leaves gone with the wind

On a naked branch of wild cherry tree

Singing and mimicking

The blue jay sound

Saying:

With all the deforestation

And with all the birds gone along with their nests

How on earth I can sing as blue jay

And still people believe in me that

Everything is just fine

No Bible: I Swear by the Thickness of Yellow Page Book Alone

A tiny bird

with coat of feather

As thin as the skin of apple

builds a modest shelter with the lover

to raise a family

Always high up

Food

Only few morsels

Survives year round all four seasons

Generation after generation

if man was not there with all of the hassle

yet the human society

with infinite needs

constantly on the rise each day

still unhappy for the fear of

The Impending Armageddon

The complete disappearance of his kind from world

Need!

I need "IT"

Now!

Rocks Holding Water Long for Birds

I

have

become so heavy

from excess weight

So much so that

When I walk on solid rock

I can see I have left

A deep engraved foot print behind on them

But Lucky birds though

Despite my indigestion

Will find water

In these leak free footprint bird bath holes

Not only for drinking

But also for self-cleansing

In the heat of summer

Bombardments

Dust of time pouring on me

It is invisible

It is undetectable

It is without trace

Dust of time pouring on me

I feel it despite being undetectable

Even in a sunny day after the snow storm

It is pouring on me

Like ashes of fire in absolute weightlessness

If there is body to light in form of subatomic particles

There is none whatsoever in the dust of time

It is riddled with continuous relentless bombardment

Piecing through both my body and soul

Regardless of what armor or shield I wear for protection

Simply from its original big bang

Nuclear blast in slow motion

There is no shelter or bunker to be built for protection

Even if you are awarded a contract

With expiration date in eternity

But How lucky those are who have friends!

During this life time in two dimensional bombardments

Do Not See

There are great moments

in life

that man has experienced

with great joy and contentment

what man should do?

Yes, he should tape them all in his brain cells

Under the File "permanent memory"

And when he is all by himself

He can reopen these files

Watching them all with closed eyes

In the movie theatre of "Feast of Mind"

As long as these tapes are stored in good condition

Man will be in no need of seeing world of ugliness

That comes by knocking on your open eyes

To enter into your soul

In utter rudeness by force

Beautiful Inscription

They came to me and they said

O sir what is that you are wearing in all white

White pants...

White Sweater...

And then a wide thick white scarf

Wrapped all around your neck like wide tie

Coming down long

All the way until few inches below your belly button

I said well in addition that they keep me warm

With minimal light clothing in windy cold day

It is actually a walking white marble stone

Waiting for you guys do some nice inscription on it

So latter on to be used as the carved up stone

To cover my resting place for the visitors

Or is it that too difficult for you too

So I must roll up my own sleeves to help myself

Process

My Poetry

Has no beginning of the end

And no end of the beginning

For to have an end

It is necessary

To start a new beginning

It is like oxygen in planet earth

It will never end

In order to require a new gas

To begin to refill the planet

To eliminate the void

Oak Leaf

Allies...

Have broken away

From their attachment to the botton of river

Free floating in parade before my eyes

In a transparent river to join the ocean

They come in variety of hairy shapes and forms in floatation

As if they are those unusual alien creatures

Depicted in American Hollywood space movies

After I was done watching

Their endless military parade

I asked myself

What has caused the break up of algae colony?

And why do the allies, like wandering asteroids

Have come to the surface to join the sea?

In response I ducted an oak leaf in floatation in parade

As a possible answer to my inquiry

Authentification

Man's values

are like submarines

their integrity is maintained

up to certain point

during the immersion

until it explodes into pieces

from the excess pressure

no doubt some submarines

are made far better than the others

specially when they surface

from the deep

happy in dance in jubilee

Like a leaping flying giant dinasorian great whale

Leaving water for babtism in giant splash

In Praise of Fasting

Besides God

there are three more deities

that you must bow to every day

One is called Lord the Breakfast,

the second is called Lord The Lunch,

and the third one is called Lord the Dinner.

Of course if you don't include the smaller deities

such as the lord the snack

Learn to avoid bowing to one of them at least once in a while

Falling into the Abyss

Powerful social movements

revolutions

are like giant whirlpool,

they suck in all sort of people into it

whether they like it not.

An intelligent thoughtful human being

makes his own calls and

his own choices and

his own shots

all on his own

to make sure

when he is in "IT"

he is in it because he wants to be in it

with all the risk and all the thrill and all its orgasm attached

therefore, thereof, therein, thereby, thereafte, and hitherto

TitIting of Colors

Man is half evil

and half god

when he looks at the flowers

in long pause

their colors

tend to tilt him toward his second half self

Yes my friends

Flowers colors

Are to stay for eternity

And they never fade away

Depite all the upheavals in our world

Brutally Cold

For Shabnam the generous

In modern contemporary life,

falling from the grace

has become more or less identical

with falling from the bank and the bank account

and the saving and the checking account and

stock portfolio, and the bonds,

and all the rest of paraphernalia

Therefore learn to be kind to one another

In oder to have at least a handle on this brutality

Toward your own well being

A kind face of man is a delivred promise of heaven for the humanity

Too close

It is a mistakes

for parents to identify themselves

with ebb or flow,

success or failure of their children

too tightly

as if they are glued together inseparable,

forgetting the fact that

once their children were born

their umbilical cords were severed asunder

to mark the independece of

man from man and

their mutual dependence on

the larger animal called society

Self Education

Man

under extreme pressure

can easily turn into

a monster beast,

Regardless of class or upbringing

unless from day one

he has told himself:

Yes baby

you have a beautiful mind

and nobody can take it away from you

It Is Time to Say Good Bye

Man in search of knowledge

all of sudden finds himself

without mom and dad

and intimate siblings

and children and spouse

and close or distant relatives

but alone pursuing

Journey Through the Filter of Mirror

I look around the room

Everything looks gloomy like an old abandoned graveyard with broken

head stones scattered

Furnitures appeard filled with smoke and dust impoverished

The flowers in blossom in perfume appeared stinky dead and fake dying

The spider webs were hanging from the ceiling

The cracked rusted old paints on walls were swelling and falling

The space was shrunk to that of a dead end with pressurizing in

suffocation

All in all the spirit of sorrow and sadness & death had taken over the

entire room

I got up

Looked again at the room but this time through the mirror

The rome replica on the other side of mirror suddenly changed in

character

Now the air inside the room is crispy and fresh breathable

The spide webs all gone with walls painted with breautiful color brand new

The space is enlarged with open vista

The spirit of sorrow and sadness had yielded into the joy and

spontaneous life

All the smokes and dust were gone by the mirror vaccum

The furnitures appeard brand new this time with glamour and awe

Yes, indeed I had travelled from the world of sorrow to the world of joy

Through and by the cleasing and glorifying gate of mirror

Truthiness

Among all the symbolisms

That stand for truth

Nothing is as powerful and as straightforward

Than the sun itself

But amongst us all the truth seekers

Who Wish to look straight onto this clear cut truthfullness

Who?

Gate

To every door, there is a key for openning;

to every dam, there is a free waterway,

and to every wall there is window;

Even in the sealed tomb of pharoh

there is an open gate way

Linking him to another world for his after life journey—

Swell

Ebbs and flow of the sea,

waves swelling and crushing the beam,

Just like the contraction and expansion of the heart,

Just like the swelling of the lungs,

all fin motion raising one major question,

for whose esteem and honor

we roll on and on & rule without the team?

When most slept wihout the mercy and without the rhyme

Happiness

There are many ways

to experience God

in most objective and tangible manner

to become cognizant of him,

the most important one, is to become aware of your own breathing

as God enters and leaves your body

even if you are in a crap hole pit

all the way up to your chin

therefore it is important for man

To have a genuine campaign

To be orchestrated toward clean air act

This year

And all the years ahead following in awaiting in the horizen

Breathe

Man breathes not just through his lungs and his skin

but also through his eyes.

Today I was inhaling

pure unpolluted & unadulterated oxygen in cold winter

by gazing at a vibrant deep red poinsettia...

yes poinsettia,

when vibrant roses

were still meditating on their roots

for their resurrection in later spring toward oxgygenation

Cheating: Taste of Woods

They have thrown me

Into the woods in blind folded ness

Yet expecting me

To paint the leaves and trees

And all the surrounding

In separate art work canvas

By relying only on

The feeling of smell I get

From the breeze

And on the sound I hear from

The creatures in the vicinity and afar

Therefore with all these limitations

I have no choice

But to cheat

That is to stick out my tongue

To taste the forest in its totality

If all the touching of surrounding

Can't give me enough clue as to what is it that

I am supposed to see

For my art work

King on the Throne

Leaves

One

After

Another

are pushed off the branches

descending ...

And as they in dance

fall gently

to touch earth

realize for first time

their source of identity

is way vast & far beyond their mother ...

Thanks to mother tree

for her austere identity education

The Fourth Way

Some people die to live in this world,

Some die to avoid this world,

And some find the middle ground between the two.

My way is the last one

For this world deserves some pride

What would be the fourth way?

Buddha Full enlightenment

The ultimate form of human consciouness

In its high apex everest

Is to become sun;

In Full and in all out continuous explusion relentlessly

Even during the time of eclips

In Memory of Drunken Ahmad

I told him

The smell of dry perfumed wood fire smoke is the greatest of all

In response he smiled

I asked him for the reason behind his mystical smile

As if there was a subliminal message

He smiled again and said the smell of freshly made food is far better

Moving to My Beverly Hills Mansion

How many times we have seen sun set and sun rise

How many times we have seen all the phases of moon

How many times we have witnessed

The coming and going of the four seasons

And the roaring of blue ocean

How many times we have observed clouds moving in blue sky

Making shapes after shapes

How many times we have noticed and heard the pouring rains

How many times we have zoomed on leaves dancing falling in fall

How many times we have seen stars at night with might

How many times we have entered and left the same house

How many times we have exchanged the same hello & how are you

How many times we traveled into night until day

Yet despite all these repetitions

We wish to see them again without novelty

Resisting Leaves

Fall ...

Leaves...

They are pushed off by mother tree

They are deprived from food

In complete disconnectedness

They have gotten heavier from constant rain

And still heavier

By the constant blowing wind around them

Yet despite all the odds

Some of the leaves holding on tight to their mother

Refusing to accept the inevitable

As they see their comrades

One after another in great numbers

Breaking ranks right before their eyes in a nose dive downfall

Atom

In autumn

Each leaf

On the tree

Is a king

But since

They do not have

Ties to soil

Like roots

Deep and deeper

They all fall

One after another

On the face of land

As they turn into powder

And then blown away

In metamorphosis

Into so many microscopic species in belittlement